8 Great WONDERS

NEW LIFE IN JESUS

LifeMission Church Edition

Table of Contents

i   Introduction—My Place in God's History with People

1   Chapter 1—**Creation and Forever**
    What does God want for every one of us?

15 Chapter 2—**Separated, Judged, and Crucified**
    Why is salvation necessary?

29 Chapter 3—**Crucifixion and Resurrection**
    How was salvation provided?

47 Chapter 4—**Spirit, Soul, and Body**
    How is friendship with God experienced?

65 Afterword—Checking and Rechecking the Connections

    Endnotes

Introduction—
MY PLACE IN GOD'S HISTORY WITH PEOPLE

"For God so loved the world, that He gave His only begotten Son, that whosoever believeth in Him should not perish, but have everlasting life."   —*John 3:16*

It's a big moment. And people use all kinds of phrases to describe it:

"I met Christ," "got saved."

"I received Jesus as my Lord and Savior."

"I made a decision for Christ," "was born again."

"I went forward," "responded to the altar call."

"I asked God to forgive my sins," "prayed the Sinner's Prayer."

"I gave my life to the Lord," "asked Jesus to come into my heart."

"I put my faith in God."

i

Or very simply, "I became a Christian."

No matter what anyone calls it, when people respond to the gospel, they do so for their own reasons.

"I invited Jesus into my life... because it was a total mess."

"I asked God to forgive me... because I was hurting, and hurting others."

"I came to Christ... because I wanted him to fix my marriage and my family."

Or even, "I accepted Jesus as my Savior... because I finally understood that he is the Son of God."

It's natural and right for salvation to start this way, but, 'our prayer' for 'our reason' is only half of the story. It's one thing for us to know why we received salvation, but do we know why God offers us salvation in the first place? I think I know what's in it for me. But what's in it for God? What does he hope to gain from this whole 'salvation-thing'?

The Bible has been described in a lot of different ways. Someone said that the letters B, I, B, L, E stand for 'Basic Instructions Before Leaving Earth.' Others have said that the Bible is God's love letter to us, and it certainly is. But for our lessons here we need to see the Bible as a record of God's history with people. What is revealed when we look at the interactions between God and humankind since the beginning?

The teaching in this book is based on something I call *8 Great Wonders*. The *8 Great Wonders* are moments the Bible talks about which summarize God's history with people. They show us what God wants for every one of us. They show us why salvation is necessary, and how salvation was provided. And they show us how friendship with God is actually experienced.

When I present the *8 Great Wonders* to people, I like to share them as news headlines.

God Created People

People Sinned Against God

God's Law Condemned Sinners

Jesus Christ Died for Sinners

Jesus, Alive Again!

People, Born Again

God's People Live by Faith

God and His People, Together Forever

The word *gospel* means 'good news,' and the good news is that God has done everything needed to be done to make it possible for each of us to know him personally.

"This is eternal life, that they may know You, the only true God, and Jesus Christ whom You have sent." —John 17:3

It's important to note, however, that the relationship God offers doesn't come from simply knowing and understanding God's side of the story from the Bible. Having eternal life, knowing God, happens when I look at "God's history with people" and see "my relationship with God."

God Created Me

I Sinned Against God

God's Law Condemned Me

Jesus Christ Died for Me

Jesus Offers Me His Life

my name **Is Born Again**

my name **Lives by Faith**

God and Me, Together Forever

When we look more closely at the *8 Great Wonders*, it becomes clear that 'friendship with God' is the main idea revealed through his history with people.

In the first chapter of this book, "Creation and Forever," we will see that God created people to be *like him*, because he wants us to *know him* and *be with him* forever.

"Separated, Judged, and Crucified" is the name of the second chapter. In it, we will learn that our sin caused our death, which is separation from God.

God was confronting our sin and death through the "Crucifixion and Resurrection," the focus of the third chapter. In it, we will understand *why* Jesus truly is the only way to God.

And in the fourth chapter, "Spirit, Soul, and Body," we will discover how God's life in us affects every part of who we are. It will become clear how we can experience a personal relationship with God every day of our lives.

So... you know why you "got right with God," or "invited Christ into your life," or "accepted salvation." But now, you may be realizing that it's time to hear more about God's side of the story. If so, the following prayer might be the best place to start.

Lord,

I'm realizing that there is something more to my salvation than I thought there was. I ask that you teach me from your word what it means for me to live as a saved person, as someone who knows you personally. I want to know you as well as I can.

In Jesus' name. Amen.

Chapter 1—
CREATION AND FOREVER

What does God want for every one of us?

> *God created us to be like him, because he wants us to know him and be with him forever.*

* * *

Principles of a Wonderful Trip

DAD. *(Gathers his wife and children for a family meeting.)* We will be taking our annual vacation four months from today. My friend Jim at work suggested that we might really enjoy Yellowstone National Park. What do you think?

FAMILY. *(Cheering in unison.)* Hooray!

(It's just a story.)

Principle #1:

Make your necessary first decisions with the destination in mind.

> **DAD.** I told Jim that we could borrow Uncle Vincent's pop-up camper and drive to Yellowstone, but he says it's a two-day drive from here. We don't want to spend four days of our vacation on the road. *(To his wife.)* Sweetheart, since you're the computer guru, I'm going to ask you to go online and make our reservations. We'll fly into Billings, Montana, and come in from the northeast. We need to book a cabin a couple of miles outside the park. And we also need to rent a hard-shell camper.
>
> **MOM.** A hard-shell camper?
>
> **DAD.** It will protect us from the bears.
>
> *(The children's eyes are as big as saucers.)*

Principle #2:

Re-adjust your priorities as the plan begins to unfold.

> *(The following morning, Mom goes over the airline itinerary and lets the family know that everything is confirmed.)*
>
> **MOM.** I can't wait for the trip. I called Aunt Maria last night and got some natural recipes to try while we're out in the wild.
>
> **DAD.** Honey, don't forget that you're on vacation, too. Besides, every moment spent cooking is a moment not spent enjoying the great outdoors.

SON. Dad, I'm saving all my money for the trip. I have $13.37 so far.

DAD. That's great, son. We're all going to have to save our money. With airline fares, cabin and camper rentals, meals out, and park fees, this trip looks to cost around $3,000. There's going to be some changes in this family's spending habits for a while.

Principle #3:
Stay committed to your decision by remembering why you've made the changes you've made.

DAD. But, sweetheart, a [*latest technological widget*] like this one has never been this cheap before. And the sale ends tomorrow.

MOM. It's only been two weeks, and you've already forgotten about Yellowstone? You know we can't afford the trip *and* a [*latest technological widget*]. You don't want to disappoint the children, do you?

DAD. You're right. And why did you have to bring the kids into it?

Principle #4:
Stay focused by talking with others who have been where you are.

MOM. Jim, we're so glad that you and Mary joined us for dinner. These last two months have been kind of tough on the kids. I was hoping you would share some stories from your past trips to Yellowstone.

JIM. Glad to. The most wonderful place on earth is called the Grand Canyon of the Yellowstone. You've never seen a rainbow until you've seen one there in the spray from the waterfalls.

SON. Mr. Lewis, I thought Old Faithful was the favorite sight in Yellowstone.

JIM. The entire park is spectacular.

DAUGHTER. Mrs. Lewis, what's your favorite sight there?

MARY. I've never seen meadows as beautiful as they are in Yellowstone. Sounds a little silly to go to the mountains and enjoy the meadows most, but they're just *filled* with elk and other kinds of wildlife.

Principle #5:

Prepare for the destination. Then prepare some more.

DAD. *(Asking his friend for advice.)* Jim, I was hoping you would look over my checklist to make sure I haven't left off anything important.

JIM. Let's have a look-see. *(Mumbles through the list.)* Camera, good. Do you have any binoculars? *(Mumbles.)* Sleeping bags. Take some extra blankets. The nights are cold whatever time of year you go. *(Mumbles.)* New boots? If you've never been hiking before I would suggest trying out some of the trails around here first. You'll get a good feel for it. Plus, you'll break in your boots. *(Mumbles through the rest of the list.)* Don't forget insect repellant and sunscreen.

DAD. Yikes, I'm glad I talked to you.

JIM. I would also suggest visiting with a Park Ranger and picking up some trail maps before you hike. You can ask about things like building campfires, and he'll talk to you about do's and don'ts. Most people are unaware of the park's dangers.

DAD. Dangers?

JIM. Yeah, a lot of injuries in the park are buffalo-related. They're really kind of mean.

Principle #6:
Enjoy the experience as the anticipation and excitement build.

MOM. Wake up, children. Today's the day.

* * *

Mission Statement

I once heard a motivational speaker[1] say, "Your direction in life must determine your decisions, or else your decisions in life will certainly determine your direction." Are you employed in the area of your college major? Most graduates cannot answer yes. So, what happened? What could help us become a voice of direction, rather than a victim of decisions?

A few individuals I know, as well as most every company I've heard of, have a mission statement. A mission statement is simply a word picture of the outcome one desires. For example, if you were in business to manufacture widgets, then your mission statement might read: *To put widgets in the homes of every family in the USA.*

Let's say the widget business is good, but to make things better, your Board of Directors recommends that the company run television spots and they believe you should star in the commercials. You look at your mission statement and the answer is obvious. You say yes.

The buying public loves seeing your face and remembers the company's name. Noting your success, someone suggests that you should also endorse products and services for other companies; actually become an actor in TV ads. *That's cool,* you think. *Fame and fortune can be mine.*

But wait a minute. Your mission statement reads: *To put 'widgets' in the homes of every family in the USA.* If this future is going to take place, you really have no choice but to say no and stay focused on widgets. Right?

Would it surprise you to know that God has a mission statement? It's really not all that complex. It's a single phrase, made up of only four words: *The kingdom of God.*

'The kingdom of God' has been God's direction since the beginning. It has been the determining factor in all of his decisions from even before he said, "Let us make man in our image" (Genesis 1:26). I believe that if we were to see God's home movies of the moment he spoke those words and we looked closely at what's in the background of the shot, we would see that God was standing in front of his kingdom. After all, Jesus Christ said that, one day, he will invite us to "Come, you who are blessed by my Father, inherit the kingdom that has been prepared for you since the foundation of the world" (Matthew 25:34). This means that the kingdom was prepared before Adam and Eve were created.

Our goal, in this chapter, is to see the connection between the first *Great Wonder*, "God Created People," and the last *Great Wonder*, "God and His People, Together Forever."

The connection can be seen more clearly if you're willing to do some homework. Within the next couple of days, I want you to read all four of these Bible chapters; Genesis 1 & 2 and Revelation 21 & 22. Read them straight through as though they make up a single story. I've often referred to it as *The What-Could-Have-Been Bible*.

Here's what I've found in the story. A key thought in the first two chapters of the Bible says that "God created mankind in his own image" (Genesis 1:27). And a key thought in the last two chapters says that "God will live with mankind, and they will be his people" (Revelation 21:3). Genesis tells us that people were created to be *like* God. Revelation tells us that people are meant to be *with* God forever.

The Bible says that Jesus preached 'the gospel of the kingdom' (Matthew 4:23, Luke 16:16). He unveiled God's plan to rescue us and to bring us back to himself. This was Jesus' message. And we, too, can live for the same purpose.

The Kingdom of God

I have a limited amount of experience in the business world. I'm not an expert of experts, but here's something I do know. *To achieve success in any endeavor, you must have a mental snapshot of the desired future which has <u>the strength to pull you</u> through the realities of today.* Keep in mind that, by itself, a snapshot of the outcome you want isn't enough. With the snapshot, there must be a strong *pull* on our life, if there's going to be any lasting impact.

When Jesus spoke of the kingdom of God, he was certainly speaking in terms of a snapshot of the future. He mentioned that we would see "Abraham, Isaac, Jacob, and all the prophets in the kingdom of God" (Luke 13:28). During the Last Supper, Jesus said, "I will never eat the Passover bread again, until it is fulfilled in the kingdom of God. I will not drink the fruit of the vine until the kingdom of God comes" (Luke 22:16, 18).

But Jesus taught people about *the pull* of the kingdom more often than he spoke of the snapshot. Let's look at what Jesus said about the kingdom of God, or the kingdom of heaven, in the context of the *Principles of a Wonderful Trip*, which is where we began the chapter.

Principle #1:
Make your necessary first decisions with the destination in mind.

... "The time is fulfilled, and the kingdom of God is at hand; repent and believe in the gospel." —Mark 1:15

... "Truly I say to you, unless you are converted and become like children, you will not enter the kingdom of heaven." —Matthew 18:3

... "Truly, truly, I say to you, unless one is born again he cannot see the kingdom of God." —John 3:3

Listen to the concepts behind these Bible words.

Repent — Turn 180° and begin to move in God's direction.

Believe in the gospel — Buy into the message of God's mission.

Be converted — Be changed.

Become like children — Start fresh.

How is all of this possible?

Be born again — Accept God's offer to replace the emptiness inside us with his kind of life.

Remember, if we don't purchase tickets for our vacation getaway, the travel brochure is all we will ever experience.

Principle #2:

Re-adjust your priorities as the plan begins to unfold.

"But seek first his kingdom and his righteousness, and all these things [food, water, and clothing] *will be added to you."*
          —Matthew 6:33

29... "Truly I say to you, there is no one who has left house or wife or brothers or parents or children, for the sake of the kingdom of God, 30who will not receive many times as much at this time and in the age to come, eternal life."
          —Luke 18:29–30

Look at the deal God offers: *Make my kingdom your top priority, and I'll make your life my top priority.* In essence, he's asking us to adopt his mission statement as our own. It's simple, but not easy. And we'll never buy into making this adjustment until we believe it's worth it. In many of the parables he told, Jesus spoke like it is.

Principle #3:
Stay committed to your decision by remembering why you've made the changes you've made.

... *"No one, after putting his hand to the plow and looking back, is fit for the kingdom of God."* —*Luke 9:62*

But interestingly...

"Do not be afraid, little flock, for your Father has chosen gladly to give you the kingdom." —*Luke 12:32*

The destination is established and our priorities are outlined. But afterward, we only manage to muster a half-commitment. And I'm not even talking about Christianity! We're less-than-committed in our jobs, in our friendships, in life in general. It's human nature. So, from the verses above, we see that Jesus addressed our human nature with a very harsh statement: *Anything less than 100% commitment is unacceptable.* But then, he also reminded us that this whole kingdom idea is based on God's generosity and his love for us.

Principle #4:
Stay focused by talking with others who have been where you are.

"Blessed are the poor in spirit, for theirs is the kingdom of heaven." —*Matthew 5:3*

"Blessed are those who have been persecuted for the sake of righteousness, for theirs is the kingdom of heaven."

—*Matthew 5:10*

When we experience a change of heart for the better, we're tempted later to change our mind. Initial decisions are often followed by internal doubt. Likewise, the pull of the kingdom in our life, even over the long haul, will be challenged by the push to keep us down.

What is it that will help us overcome the weight on our shoulders?

It's been my experience that the stories and fellowship of others who are on the same path provide the greatest encouragement to keep moving forward. That's when I see the destination all over again. That's when I feel the blessing of kingdom life.

Principle #5:
Prepare for the destination. Then prepare some more.

"Not everyone who says to me, 'Lord, Lord,' will enter the kingdom of heaven, but he who does the will of my Father who is in heaven will enter."   —*Matthew 7:21*

... "Therefore every scribe who has become a disciple of the kingdom of heaven is like a head of a household, who brings out of his treasure things new and old."   —*Matthew 13:52*

... "To you it has been granted to know the mysteries of the kingdom of heaven."   —*Matthew 13:11*

Let's say we're in Paris and we can only speak English. Is it more realistic to expect Parisians to stop speaking French around us, or to find an interpreter?

11

Welcome to Kingdom Speak 101. Since knowing the local language of our destination increases our participation and enjoyment of the local culture, let's begin learning the language of the kingdom. The following is a list of phrases spoken by Jesus. I call them *Jesus Verbs*[2]:

Believe me, follow me, practice the truth,
Worship, let your light shine, freely give, love me,
Keep my word, pray and fast, ask/seek/knock,
Take courage, come to me, hear my words/act on them,
Forgive, take up your cross, humble yourself,
Hear my voice, serve others,
Count the cost, keep watching and praying,
Receive the Holy Spirit, shepherd my sheep,
Go/preach/make disciples/baptize them/teach them

Experiencing the customs and culture of God's kingdom now will prepare us for life in His kingdom later. And our embracing of the *Jesus Verbs* will quite naturally be accompanied by the pull of the kingdom in our life.

Principle #6:
Enjoy the experience as the anticipation and excitement build.

Here's the amazing thing about the trip. It's different for all of us. I've intentionally skipped over scriptures for this principle because our own journey will be completely unique and different from anyone else's. For this principle, I don't want us to focus on biblical commonality, but rather, on a *personal* friendship with God.

And let me say this: Even though the trip is personal, we don't have to keep it to ourselves. It's okay to tell others about it. It's okay to take others with us.

You know, it's likely that someone will ask us how we can believe in a kingdom none of us has ever seen. But if we've seen the pull of the kingdom in the lives of other people and it has strengthened the pull in our own lives, then it's not difficult to believe at all.

*   *   *

The Pull in One Man's Life

The late Charlie Ragus had a huge impact on my life. Most of what I've learned about personal development and leadership I learned through my association with one of the companies he founded. I believe that, through his influence, he helped prepare me for the work I've done as a writer and teacher.

Charlie was a wonderful storyteller. The last time I saw him, he held a Bible in his hand as he shared a great story of the pull in his life.

Charlie told two of his close associates, Rick and Brian, that he wanted them to join him on an important visit to a friend they all knew. The purpose, he said simply, was to share the message of Jesus Christ with this man.

Charlie grabbed his Bible as the three men left to see their friend. They flew to an unattended airstrip near a mountain where the man lived. When they got off the plane, they stood together holding hands, and prayed for the rest of their journey and for God's work to be completed in their friend's heart. Then, they drove up the mountain to their friend's home.

What would compel Charlie to go to such great lengths; a plane trip, a drive up a mountain? What could make someone feel such a sense of purpose?

Rick shared with me later[3] that "When we arrived, Charlie wasted no time in going to the heart of the matter. He walked our friend through the *Romans Road*[4] and led him in a prayer of commitment."

Charlie then joked that, since Rick was an ordained minister, he was obviously the one meant to baptize their friend in the frigid waters of a nearby river. Rick recalled with a smile that "the water in the river was only about 20 inches deep, and was around 35 degrees... it was a quick baptism." But what a moment it must have been.

I'm sure that as this dear friend felt the pull of the river's water near his home, that Charlie felt a fresh pull on his heart from the kingdom of God.

And it may seem like a stretch, but I can imagine God and Adam, just after Creation, sitting on the bank of another river, the river that flowed from the Garden of Eden[5]. As they watch the sunlight glimmer on the water, God's thoughts wander— from a river which will begin at his throne in the kingdom[6], to the icy waters that rush down the side of a mountain near the home of Charlie's friend.

Adam sees the far-away look in God's eyes. "Lord, what are you thinking about?"

He smiles. "I was thinking about how beautiful rivers can be."

Chapter 2—
SEPARATED, JUDGED, AND CRUCIFIED

Why is salvation necessary?

Our sin separated us from God. His Law judged us and sentenced us to die as sinners. And when Jesus died for us, we were "crucified with him." This is why Jesus said, "You must be born again."

---

* * *

What If?

The serpent was the craftiest animal that the Lord God made. One day it said to Eve, "C'mon, has God really said that you cannot eat from any tree in the garden?"

The woman answered, "Sure, we can eat fruit from the trees in the garden, but, about the tree that is in the middle *of the garden, God did say, 'You cannot eat from it or even touch it, or you will die.'"*

The serpent said to the woman, "You will not die! Listen, God knows that the day you eat from it your eyes will be opened and you will be just like him, knowing good and evil."

The woman saw that the tree produced good food, that it was beautiful to look at, and that it could make her wise¹ **... but, together with her husband, she told the serpent no.**

The man and his wife heard the sound of the Lord God walking in the garden in the cool of the day² ... and they ran to be with him.

What if, in that most decisive moment in human history, the decision had been made to resist temptation and to obey God?

If that were the case, then maybe Cain doesn't murder Abel. God doesn't destroy the world with a flood. And Sodom and Gomorrah still remain, to this day, as cities of righteousness rather than bywords of wretchedness.

Between the first two chapters in the Bible, which tell of God's creation, and the last two, which tell of his kingdom, there are 1,185 chapters. As though situated between parentheses, they tell of the catastrophe of sin and its solution. But if there was no sin that separated us from God, then there would be no Law that condemned us and no Crucifixion. There would be no need for them. The very chapters in the Bible that speak of these events would be gone.

It's not just Bible stories that would be affected. Many events from secular history would also be erased. There would be no Trojan Horse, no Alexander the Great, no Ides of March. There would be no Holy War, no Genghis Khan, no Black Death, and no Conquistadores. There would be no Ivan the Terrible, no Calcutta's 'Black Hole,' no Zulu's 'Blood River.' There would be no American Civil War, no Battle of Little Bighorn. There would be no Bloody Sunday, no War to End War, no Bolsheviks. There would be no Hitler, no Holocaust, no Pearl Harbor, and no Hiroshima. And there would be no terrorist attacks on September 11th, 2001.

And what about our own personal histories? Think about this for a moment; no pain we've caused, no heartaches we've experienced. No skeletons in the closet, no bondages, no fear. Right now we would be experiencing peace and tranquility in God's kingdom, where lions lay down with lambs. God's face would be the first thing we saw this morning. His voice, the last thing we hear before we sleep at night.

Of course, all of this is difficult... well, all of this is *impossible* to imagine because Eve didn't say no. She and Adam didn't run to be with God.

* * *

Crime and Punishment

At two minutes after nine, on the morning of April 19th, 1995, a bomb destroyed the Alfred P. Murrah Federal Building in Oklahoma City, Oklahoma. About 90 minutes later, Timothy McVeigh was arrested on a firearms charge during a routine traffic stop. Two days later, only hours before he was expected to make bail on the weapons charge, Federal authorities arrested McVeigh in connection with the explosion that killed 168 people, including 19 children. Less than four months later, a Federal grand jury indicted McVeigh (along with Terry Nichols) on murder and conspiracy charges.

With his arrest and indictment, McVeigh was *separated* from the society against which he had committed his crimes.

McVeigh's trial took place about two years after his arrest. The amount of evidence brought against him was absolutely staggering. The trial lasted two months and resulted in McVeigh being convicted on all 11 murder and conspiracy counts against him. On June 13th, 1997, the jury condemned McVeigh to die, and on August 14th he was formally sentenced to death.

With his conviction and sentencing, McVeigh was *condemned* to die by the laws of the society against which he had committed his crimes.

McVeigh argued that since the government claimed his victims were "not just the dead but America itself," then the country should be allowed to witness his punishment. "I am going to demand they televise it nationally," he said. That did not happen. On June 21st, 2001, McVeigh died by lethal injection. McVeigh's last statement is said to be from the poem *Invictus*[3] by William Ernest Henley.

It matters not how strait the gate,
How charged with punishments the scroll,
I am the master of my fate:
I am the captain of my soul.

When McVeigh was *executed*, the penalty was paid in full and justice was granted to the society against which he had committed his crimes.

* * *

We Have a Problem

Wow. And our Bible study started out so positively. We began by talking about how relationship is revealed through God's history with people—the *8 Great Wonders*. In Chapter 1, we looked at the connection between the first *Great Wonder* and the eighth, and we saw a future kingdom that can have a positive pull in our lives today. Now, suddenly, we're talking about crime and punishment, sin and its consequence. Especially its consequence.

The Bible refers to us, before we've accepted God's salvation, as people who are dead. "We're dead in our trespasses and sins" (Ephesians 2:1). "We're alienated, or excluded, from the life of God" (Ephesians 4:18). The Bible says that "the gospel is preached to those who are dead" (1 Peter 4:6).

If I could offer evidence which might show this to be true, I would ask an atheist to stand here beside me. I'm sure he would tell us that he has never, in any way, experienced God in his life. He might tell us that he has never seen God, heard God, smelled, tasted, or touched God. He could tell us in all sincerity that he has drawn a conclusion; that the lack of sensory evidence is one of the proofs that there is no God.

The interesting thing about this is that the Bible agrees with our friend when he says he hasn't experienced God. But the Bible offers a different reason. It isn't because God doesn't exist. It's because that part of us which was created in the image of God, created to be like God, is dead—separated from Him. And death is a consequence.

We're about to see in this chapter that our "death" before God is the connection between the second, third, and fourth *Great Wonders*: "People Sinned Against God," "God's Law Condemned Sinners," and "Jesus Christ Died for Sinners."

The Death Process

To really see this connection, we're going to look at three specific Bible verses from the Book of Romans; a mini-Bible study if you will.

The Book of Romans is actually a letter written by a man named Paul to the Christians who lived in Rome. Paul was an Apostle of Jesus Christ, although he didn't believe in Jesus when the Christian church began. He hated Christianity and persecuted its first believers. But Jesus revealed himself to Paul in an astounding way and turned him around 180°. Paul became a great influence in the Christian church, and he used his letter to the Romans as an opportunity to help people understand God's plan for us.

He begins by saying that we can certainly know there is a God, because of what we see in nature[4]. But he admits that we wouldn't know this by looking at human nature[5]. We've fallen dramatically short of the lives we're meant to live[6]. We are sinners who need a savior. Paul explains to the Christians in Rome, and to us as well, that we're dead. And he tells us when it all began.

... through one man [Adam] sin entered into the world, and death through sin, and so death spread to all men, ...

—Romans 5:12

We can ask any number of knowledgeable Christians what the word *death* means in this verse and we'll hear a consistent answer: *Death is separation from God.* Part of the punishment for Adam and Eve's disobedience was being kicked out of the Garden of Eden[7]. Worse than that, God also removed his presence, as they had known it, from the earth. They had walked and talked with him, side-by-side. And I'm sure we would all agree; we have no clue what that might have been like, having never experienced anything close to it.

Death *is* separation from God, but that's not the end of the matter. Paul went on to say that "death reigned from Adam to Moses, even over people who didn't commit Adam's sin" (Romans 5:14). He specifically said "from Adam to Moses." He also said that "sin isn't judged when there is no law" (Romans 5:13). References to *Moses* and *the Law* lead to the second verse I want us to consider:

I was once alive apart from the Law; but when the commandment came, sin became alive and I died;

—Romans 7:9

"When the commandment came... I died?"

This statement comes only 41 verses after the previous one we looked at, Romans 5:12. "Through Adam... death spread to all men."

Keep in mind that we aren't pulling scriptures from just anywhere in the Bible. These verses are in the same letter from the same writer to the same people.

Is this the same separation? Did God's Law condemn us to a death we already experienced in Adam? No. The Law did not sentence us to be separated. It doomed us to be destroyed. It may be surprising to learn that each one of the Ten Commandments can be found in the Bible with a death penalty clause attached.

Many people hold on to God's Law like it's a rulebook for life. We believe that the Law will shape our personal morality, although we often see a different result in the lives of those who hold on to it the tightest. Time and again, we find people who have become paralyzed by guilt and shame. Or we find judgmental people who have become filled with self-righteousness. This happens because God's Law does not have the effect of a rulebook on us, but rather, the effect of a courtroom. The Law condemns us all to die as sinners, and it leads us to the death we find in the final verse from Romans that we'll take a look at.

... our old self was crucified with [Christ], ...   —*Romans 6:6*

So in light of these three scriptures—here's the big question—at what point did we die?

A. In Adam—*through one man*
B. Through the Law—*when the commandment came*
C. With Christ
    Or maybe:
D. All of the above

I remember my reaction when I first heard that someone had been arrested in the Oklahoma City bombing. I thought, *If the Federal Government thinks it has a case against this guy, he's a dead man.* Was Timothy McVeigh dead while he was jailed? No. But, looking back, he was as good as dead. He was on the path and there was no turning back... just like it was for the whole human race; 'jailed' and separated from God once Adam sinned.

When I heard that the prosecution against McVeigh had millions of pieces of evidence[8], I was stunned. *This guy is absolutely dead. They're going to bury him six 'hundred' feet under.* So when the jury condemned him, was he dead? Not yet. But death was coming. It was inevitable... just like it was for all of us sinners after our 'trial and conviction,' when Moses brought the stone tablets down from the mountain.

I was sitting in my car, listening to news coverage of McVeigh's execution on the radio. And I remember the announcement that he was finally dead.

Paul makes an announcement in the Bible. "The love of God compels me to preach," he says, "because I am convinced that if Jesus Christ died for everybody,"—here's the announcement—"everybody died" (2 Corinthians 5:14). This is why we're not born into the world already experiencing a relationship with God. It doesn't happen automatically. In clear terms, this is why people *must* be born again. The emptiness inside us is directly connected to Jesus' death on our behalf. So we have no choice but to consider ourselves "crucified with Christ."

Convinced and Compelled

This belief that "everybody died" when Jesus died for us had a profound effect on Paul. He was 'convinced' and 'compelled' by it.

Paul traveled thousands of miles preaching the message of salvation through Jesus in cities where no one had ever heard it before[9]. Take a look at *Paul's Missionary Journeys* in the section of maps that can be found in many Bibles. He endured terrible hardships during his travels, saying they were proof that he was a servant of Christ[10]. Paul wrote:

> [24]*Five times I received from the Jews thirty-nine lashes.*
> [25]*Three times I was beaten with rods, once I was stoned, three times I was shipwrecked, a night and a day I have spent in the deep.* [26]*I have been on frequent journeys, in dangers from rivers, dangers from robbers, dangers from my countrymen, dangers from the Gentiles, dangers in the city, dangers in the wilderness, dangers on the sea, dangers among false brethren;* [27]*I have been in labor and hardship, through many sleepless nights, in hunger and thirst, often without food, in cold and exposure.* [28]*Apart from such external things, there is the daily pressure on me of concern for all the churches.* —2 Corinthians 11:24–28

After the first hardship, I think most of us would have been questioning whether this was really the ministry God wanted for us.

Much of Paul's second letter to the Corinthian church was written with ministry in mind. He raised the idea of ministry, in a general sense, in Chapter 3. He made it personal in

Chapter 4 when he wrote, "Since we have this ministry ... we do not lose heart" (4:1). "We are afflicted in every way, but not crushed; perplexed, but not despairing; persecuted, but not forsaken; struck down, but not destroyed; always carrying about in the body the dying of Jesus, so that the life of Jesus also may be manifested in our body" (4:8–10). In Chapter 5, Paul addressed the accusation that he must be crazy for doing what he was doing. "If we are beside ourselves, it is for God; if we are of sound mind, it is for you" (5:13).

In the very next breath, Paul tells us why he did what he did and endured what he endured. It was because of what he believed.

> *For the love of Christ controls us, having concluded this,*
> *that one died for all, therefore all died;*   *—2 Corinthians 5:14*

This verse is one of eight verses in the New Testament which associate our death directly with Christ's death for us[11]. When we understand that "our death" is tied to Adam *and* The Law *and* The Cross of Jesus, we see a much bigger issue to deal with. It's not just that one day in the future we'll stand before God and be judged, with a possibility of being damned to a lake that burns with fire and brimstone. That's true, but the Bible refers to that outcome as "the Second Death" (Revelation 20:14–15). Our immediate issue is that we already have the effects of death inside us. We've already been separated, judged, and crucified. And "unless we're born again, we will not see the kingdom of God" (John 3:3).

When I understood this truth, it changed everything for me. I didn't think any more in terms of: *When I'm lonely, I need Jesus the Friend. When I'm sick, I need Jesus the*

Healer. The poor need Jesus the Provider. The addicted need Jesus the Liberator. I realized that these conditions are symptoms of a bigger root cause. Dead people need life, and living people need healthy relationships. All people need Jesus—period.

* * *

What Do These Two People Need?

Scott was a really decent guy. He was a hard worker and a good friend. He loved his children. He cared deeply for his wife. The way he lived his life, I would have thought that Scott was a Christian. He did go to church when he was younger, but he wasn't attending church at this time in his life. He had questions about things he didn't understand and I was doing my best to give him some food for thought.

Judy, on the other hand, attended church faithfully. She had been a member of a good church for quite a number of years and had experienced the best that church life has to offer. But Judy had grown to be a bitter and angry person, and took it out on anyone who was nearby.

Judy and I worked in a mailroom. I remember sitting there together one day. We were focused on our jobs and had been silent for a while. Out of nowhere Judy started ranting and raving at God. She was looking at me, but yelling at him. When she calmed down for a moment, I responded, "Judy, all I said was good morning." She laughed, and the moment was wide-open for us to talk about some pretty tough issues.

I had been talking with Judy and Scott, individually, for several weeks when I realized something significant. I didn't know for sure whether either one of them was really a Christian. I began praying, *Holy Spirit, show me what these two people need.* And I sensed that the answer came from this question: Has anything ever been said that indicates a personal friendship with God?

I thought about Scott first. He had a church background and was a decent person, but he had never said anything that indicated that God was working in his life or that God had ever spoken to him. He had never talked in those terms. I sensed the Holy Spirit saying, *You need to share the gospel with Scott for the first time in his life.* A week later, a friend and I met with Scott over lunch. I shared the gospel with him, and he realized his need to be born again to begin his friendship with God. We had the privilege of praying with him as he accepted Jesus as his Savior and Lord. Scott began to grow as a Christian after that.

I also thought about the same question in regard to Judy. Had she ever said anything that indicated a personal friendship with God? And quite honestly, she had. She had shared a story with me.

In essence, one of her daughters was involved in a harmful lifestyle. The Holy Spirit had directed Judy to write a firm but loving letter to her daughter. She did exactly that, thinking the letter would impact her daughter. She believed that the young woman would turn away from her sin and that the two of them would be closer than they had ever been before. Unfortunately, just the opposite happened. Judy's daughter decided to stop communicating and Judy was angry about it. In her eyes, God was responsible for the broken relationship. God was mean and he really didn't care about her.

The fact that Judy had been directed by the Holy Spirit showed me that she really did have a relationship with God. Her issues had more to do with wrong perceptions of her heavenly Father and the relationship they shared.

I gave her a copy of a book which had changed my life[12]. She read the book and was also impacted. One day, I was sitting in an office surrounded by other employees. All of the sudden, Judy flew around the corner, shouting with joy, "Hey, I've been worshipping the wrong God! He loves me and I understand that now!" Part of me wanted to crawl under the desk from embarrassment, but the better part of me wanted to shout *hallelujah* from the rooftop with her.

Here's the lesson I learned from my experiences with Scott and Judy. The question of 'relationship' is what reveals whether there's life or deadness inside us.

You know, if I had focused on Scott's goodness and decency, I don't know that he would have ever come to faith in Christ. If I had focused on Judy's bitterness and anger, and tried to 'save' her again, I doubt that she would have ever returned to the loving Father she had known in her earlier years.

Chapter 3—
CRUCIFIXION AND RESURRECTION
How was salvation provided?

Jesus Christ is the Son of God. His death on the cross made
it possible for us to experience reconciliation with God and
forgiveness. His resurrection is proof that we can be born
again. Jesus is, therefore, our only way to God.

* * *

Jesus Christ is the central figure in Christianity. And right
in the middle of the *8 Great Wonders* are the fourth wonder,
"Jesus Christ Died for Sinners," and the fifth wonder, "Jesus,
Alive Again!"

I can imagine Jesus standing between these two
headlines. With one foot in front of the cross, he points
toward the first three wonders, and says, "I died for you
because you were created to be God's friend, but sin separated

you from him. I died for you because the Law condemned you to die." Then, with the other foot in front of the empty tomb, he points in the direction of the last three wonders, saying, "I rose from the dead, so that you can be born again, so that you can live by faith in the power of the Holy Spirit. I rose from the dead because you are meant to be with God forever."

The goal of this chapter is to present the connection between the fourth and fifth *Great Wonders* without lulling us all into a sense of 'been there, done that.' After all, the stories of Jesus' death and resurrection have been told millions of times; from Easter Sunday services, to passion plays and Hollywood movies. (The first motion picture featuring a portrayal of Jesus was made in 1897.)

We're going to see the connection between these events, arguably the greatest of the *Great Wonders*, from a logical, practical perspective. And this is where things get risky. Some adopt a mentality about the death and resurrection of Jesus which seems to say "you don't have to understand; you just have to believe." But we're going to take the risk. And maybe by looking at *how* we can have a relationship with God, we'll be moved emotionally by the reason *why* we can have this relationship.

The Most Offensive Words Ever Spoken

It's one thing to be controversial; it's quite another to be offensive. Certain statements made by Jesus qualify for each category.

The night before he was crucified, Jesus had an interesting conversation with his Apostles. He spent time trying to prepare them for what would take place later that night, into the next day, and beyond. Jesus told them that he would be leaving to prepare a place for them in his Father's house. He said that he would also be coming back for them so that they could be with him. Controversy surrounds statements like this.

Jesus continued by telling the men, "You know the way to get there."

One of them responded, "We don't even know where you are going. How do we know the way to get there?"

Many of us may be familiar with Jesus' answer. "I am the way, the truth, and the life," he said. "No one comes to the Father except through me" (John 14:6).

Jesus claimed to be the only way to God. For some people, these words are some of the most offensive ever spoken. "How can Jesus Christ be the *only* way? There are many world religions, many ways to get to God. After all, don't all religions teach the same thing basically?"

What Was Jesus' Claim Based On?

I can certainly understand why Jesus' words rub people the wrong way. Jesus was a teacher, just like many others. His lessons and parables are well-known, even to those among us who wouldn't consider themselves to be his followers. Many people are familiar with sayings of Jesus; like "turn the other cheek" (Matthew 5:39) and "judge not, that you be not judged" (Matthew 7:1). When people are called on to recite *The Lord's Prayer*[1] together, it always amazes me that even the most irreligious people join right in. Many people would raise their hands if they were asked, "Who knows the story of *Jesus Feeds Five Thousand*[2], or *The Parable of the Good*

31

*Samaritan*³, or *The Parable of the Prodigal Son*⁴?" And for those of us who watch sports on television, we've probably seen the big card that reads 'John 3:16.' This refers to the most well-known words Jesus ever spoke: "For God so loved the world, that he gave his only begotten Son, that whosoever believeth in him should not perish, but have everlasting life."

Even non-Christians go as far as to say that Jesus was a *great* teacher. They recognize that his teachings have influenced the world for 2,000 years. But let's be honest. He wasn't the only teacher to affect the human race. Here are a few of the other influential ones.

- Siddhartha Gautama (The Buddha)—*Indian philosopher and founder of Buddhism*
- Confucius—*Chinese philosopher*
- Socrates, Plato, and Aristotle—*Greek philosophers*
- Muhammad—*Arab prophet and founder of Islam*

And this is by no means a comprehensive list. Even in contemporary times, we've learned lessons of passive resistance and civil rights from the Mahatma Gandhi and Martin Luther King, Jr.

However, when it comes to Jesus Christ, we need to understand that he did not make his claim to be the only way to God based on his great teaching ability or even on the lessons he taught. He made his claim based on two other abilities: his ability to be God's sacrifice for the sins of all humanity, and his ability to then give anyone who will receive it the salvation we so desperately need.

In this chapter, we aren't going to compare Jesus to other moral teachers. We're simply going to look at the answers to two questions.

1. How was Jesus Christ more qualified to "die for the sins of the world" than anyone else?
2. How did Jesus demonstrate his ability to give every person the salvation they need?

If the Bible doesn't answer either of these questions, then Christianity completely unravels.

"How was Jesus more qualified to 'die for the sins of the world' than anyone else?"

In the 1980s, there was a movie called *The Last Temptation of Christ*. This controversial story depicts Jesus being tempted with thoughts of giving up on God's plan and embracing a normal life with a wife and family. I'm sure that the idea was to portray Jesus as someone who was just like us. However, we already knew that from the Bible. Hebrews 4:15 says that "Jesus was tempted in every way that we are, yet without sinning."

"Time out, pal! Didn't we discover from our mini-Bible study in the last chapter that, because of Adam, 'sin and death spread to all men'? How is it possible that Jesus was exempt from this truth?"

That's a good question. It makes sense that if Adam's sin and death spread to all people, then it began by spreading to Cain and Abel and the rest of Adam's children first. Each of the generations that followed contaminated the next. This means that a sinful and dying Noah passed sin and death on to his three sons. And a sinful and dying Abraham...

Actually, let's open the Bible to the first verses in the first book of the New Testament—the Gospel of Matthew. (Go ahead. Really do this.) Let's follow the entire list of fathers and sons presented there, starting with verse two, and say, *"this father* (Abraham) passed sin and death to *this son* (Isaac), and *this father* (Isaac) passed sin and death to *this son* (Jacob)"* Let's do this, over and over.

Our statement would be true for 40 generations, but then, at the end of the list, the wording changes with a man named Joseph. Look at verse 16. *Joseph* [was] *the husband of Mary, by whom Jesus was born.* We discover the reason for the change in wording as we read the story of the baby Jesus in the rest of the chapter[5].

Somehow we started out with a question that has Good Friday/Easter implications: *How was Jesus qualified to die for our sins?* And now we find ourselves in the Christmas story. *Jesus was born of a virgin.*

If the medical experts of his day were able to run a paternity blood test on Jesus, what would they have discovered? They would have found that Jesus did not have Joseph's blood running through his veins. He did not have his mother Mary's blood running through his veins either.

From the book *The Chemistry of the Blood* by M. R. DeHaan, M.D.[6]:

> The mother provides the fetus (the unborn developing infant) with the nutritive elements for the building of that little body in the secret of her womb, but all the blood which forms in it is formed in the embryo

itself. From the time of conception to the time of birth of the infant not one single drop of blood ever passes from mother to child. The placenta, that mass of temporary tissue known better as "afterbirth," forming the link between mother and child, is so constructed that although all the soluble nutritive elements such as proteins, fats, carbohydrates, salts, minerals and even antibodies pass freely from mother to child and the waste products of the child's metabolism are passed back to the mother's circulation, no actual interchange of a single drop of blood ever occurs normally. All the blood which is in that child is produced within the child itself.

Jesus Christ was sinless, and qualified to "die for the sins of the world" because he was the only begotten—which means *physically fathered*—Son of God. He was exempt from Adam's sin and death because he wasn't fathered by a descendant of Adam, but by God. He literally had God's blood running through his veins.

The Bible makes a big deal about the blood of Jesus. It says that "we've been justified" (Romans 5:9), "we have redemption" (Ephesians 1:7), and "we've been purchased with his blood" (Revelation 5:9). It says that the blood of Jesus "cleanses us from all sin" (1 John 1:7). Someone may respond, "That all sounds like cryptic, symbolic Bible language. Weren't we going to talk in logical and practical terms?"

Buckle up.

The writer of the New Testament Book of Hebrews (a letter to the Jewish people) compares Jesus' death for our sins with the system of animal sacrifices that we see clearly and tragically in the Old Testament (see Hebrews 9:1–10:18). He reminds his Jewish readers that the high priest went into the Most Holy Place one time a year to offer blood on behalf of the people (9:7), but that Jesus went directly into the presence of God in heaven one time in history to offer his blood for everyone (9:12). The blood of bulls and goats only "covered over" previously committed sins, but blood of Jesus completely "takes away" all sins... for all time. The writer tells us that the Old Testament sacrificial system was "copies of the things in the heavens" but that Jesus' death was "the heavenly things themselves" (9:23).

The sacrificing of animals really is cruel and tragic. But I believe God wanted us to feel the heart-wrenching emotion of an innocent dying for the guilty. I don't think we were supposed to grow calloused toward it. If we can feel the unfairness of the 'copy,' maybe we can begin to see the horrific significance of Jesus' sacrifice for the sin in *our* lives. If we could even scratch the surface of 'the innocent dying for the guilty,' maybe, just maybe, we could begin to understand the great love that God has for us.

"For God so loved the world, that he gave his only begotten Son ..."

The *Why* Behind the *How*

Hopefully, we understand that Christianity isn't based on things that we have to pretend are true. Hopefully, the *how* of how a relationship with God is possible makes sense. But then again, it's really not about the how. It's about the *why*. So, let's ask why. Why did the sinless Son of God willingly bleed and die on a cross?

God's love for us is also called 'grace.' God's grace is not a romantic, daydreaming kind of love. It is extreme love in action. It is love to the rescue. I can't imagine a greater definition for grace than this: "For God so loved the world, that he gave his only begotten Son, that whosoever believeth in him should not perish, but have everlasting life." And I can't imagine a greater demonstration of God's grace for us either.

Notice that the verse doesn't say *for God so loved the plan*. The message of the gospel isn't about the plan as much as it's about the love that God feels in his heart for *us*. The very day Jesus died, God was thinking very specifically about you and me.

Take a look at 2 Corinthians 5:19, which begins "God was in Christ, reconciling the world to himself." In the last chapter we saw a death process which began when Adam and Eve disobeyed God. With sin came separation from God. But separation is reversed by reconciliation. In Christ, God ended the world's separation from himself.

The verse goes on to say that God is "no longer holding our sins against us"—a great definition of forgiveness. The second part of the death process we looked at was condemnation. We were condemned by the Law to die as sinners. But condemnation is nullified by forgiveness. In Christ, God released the condemnation hanging over our lives.

The word *gospel* means 'good news.' And the good news is this: When Jesus died on the cross for you and me, God reconciled us to himself and forgave us completely. Think about it. God is with us right now and he isn't holding anything in his heart against us.

37

"Are you sure that's the way God thinks of me, that He's close to me and isn't holding anything against me, because it really doesn't *feel* that way." Unfortunately, that's true. It doesn't feel that way.

Imagine this. Two people are the best of friends. They do everything together. We'd say that they're inseparable. But something happens and one betrays the other. They part ways. They live completely separate lives for many years. One day, news comes that the betrayer has died and the other feels compelled to attend the funeral, where he breaks down emotionally. He falls against the casket and cries, "I'm here! I'm here!" Through his tears, he sobs, "I love you. I forgive you. I want us to be friends again." But the dead man can't respond.

God, in essence, is leaning over our casket. And he's very passionately speaking these same words to us. Reconciliation and forgiveness really did become fully available to us the day Jesus died on the cross, but because of the deadness inside us, we can't even comprehend these spiritual realities.

"How did Jesus demonstrate his ability to give every person the salvation they need?"

Thankfully, God can do for us what the broken-hearted man only wishes he could do for his friend. God can give us life through the same power that brought his only begotten Son back to life. Through the power of the Holy Spirit, who raised Jesus from the dead, we can be recreated in the image of God. That's what the phrase *born again* means. Rather than feeling separated from God, we can experience a reconciled relationship. Rather than thinking that he is condemning us, we can know his forgiveness and grace... once we've dealt with the issue of our death before God.

Jesus died for our sins; his crucifixion is ours. He demonstrated power over death by rising from the dead; his life can be our resurrection.

Is there another great moral teacher who was conceived by the Holy Spirit and born of a virgin, who died for the sins of the whole world, whose resurrection demonstrated his or her power to give people life? If there is, then maybe there is another way to get to God. But if not, it doesn't do us any good to stay offended at Jesus' claim to be the only way.

I think of my friend Craig's story. He was skeptical about Christianity, although his wife had been a Christian for several years and was a part of our ministry's early brainstorming sessions. Because Craig and I are personal friends, he accompanied his wife to many of these meetings, and for a few months he heard the message over and over. One day he called me during his drive home from work.

"You know, this sounds completely crazy to me. But when you say that God talks to you, that you have a relationship with him, I believe you. I really do. But it brings up a nagging question. Why hasn't God ever spoken to me?" We visited for about a half an hour and talked about the very things we've looked at in the first chapters of this book.

I told him about the eight events that combine to form the story of God's history with people, and I shared the events as headlines.

I said, "Craig, I've learned that the salvation God offers does not result from us knowing and understanding the details of God's story only. We are saved when we make 'God's history with people' 'my relationship with God'."

God Created Me

I Sinned Against God

God's Law Condemned Me

Jesus Christ Died for Me

Jesus Offers Me His Life

my name **Is Born Again**

my name **Lives by Faith**

God and Me, Together Forever

I asked Craig, "Is this what you want? Do you want to begin your friendship with God? Are you willing to follow Jesus—the only way to God—by turning 180° from the sin in your life, and experiencing God's grace and forgiveness? The Holy Spirit will live inside you, changing your character and giving you the power to live with meaning and purpose. Is all of this what you want?"

Craig told me that he needed time to process the information I had shared. And he did exactly that. I had the privilege of being with Craig just one week later as he prayed from his heart, committing his life to the Lord Jesus. Some people will read this book and sense a readiness right now to do the same. Is this the case for you?

If so, I'm going to ask you to do something which may seem strange and a bit uncomfortable. I'm about to ask you to stop reading and begin praying. Now you know about the salvation that's necessary to experience the relationship that's available. Now it's time to talk to God about it. The following questions may help prompt you as you pray your own personal prayer to God. After each point, stop and pray.

- *Do you feel distant from God and guilty for your sin? Do you feel the Holy Spirit prompting you to receive God's forgiveness and friendship? Respond to God in your own words.*

- *Are you thankful that Jesus paid your death penalty? Do you believe that God raised Jesus from the dead and can bring life to you as well? Express your belief. Ask God to answer your questions and doubts.*

- *Do you want to become all that God wants you to be? Are you willing to give up control of your life, to follow the leading of the Holy Spirit? Offer a declaration of surrender. Welcome the Holy Spirit into your life.*

- *Are there any personal issues that you would like to talk to God about? Share from your heart. He wants to 'know you' because you want him to know you.*

* * *

Celebration for a Life

People accept salvation through Jesus Christ for various reasons, but the ultimate result should be the beginning of a relationship with God. I remember a night when I refused to do something good but difficult that the Holy Spirit had asked me to do. I felt so bad about my disobedience afterward that I made a promise to God. *Lord, from now on I'll do whatever you ask me to do. I'll never disobey you again.* This should be our prayer of commitment to God when we start, rather than when we blow it, like I did.

There are times when we can describe our life as a Christian as 'my questions and God's answers.' On other occasions, it will be 'God's initiative and my response.' Either way, God is the source of what's best for us. And it's our obedience to what he wants which actually leads to our best life. Christians are 'followers of Jesus,' and built right into this new life of ours is a first act of obedience—being baptized in water.

Baptism doesn't add more to our salvation, but it's very important and powerful. It symbolizes our death, burial, and resurrection with Christ. Now it's true that all people are born into this world living under the effects of death and burial, but we haven't experienced the resurrection of Jesus until we commit our lives to him and are born again. Therefore, baptism is a symbolic, public showing of a completed cycle: from created in the image of God, to crucified with Christ, to recreated in the image of God. In essence, baptism says, "Let everyone know and understand that I am now complete in Jesus Christ!"

People have been baptized in several traditional ways, but I love the symbolism of our "burial through baptism" mentioned in Romans 6:4, so I choose to immerse, or dunk people completely underwater.

I've baptized people in various places: from an outdoor hot tub in the month of January, to the baptismal tank of the First Baptist Church my grandparents attended. Together, my wife and I baptized our daughter in a junior high swimming pool, surrounded by church friends. God isn't concerned about where someone is baptized as much as he is about our declaration to others and the experience of his presence.

I baptized a woman in her aunt and uncle's backyard Jacuzzi. She had been a Christian for a while, but had never experienced this wonderful symbol of her faith in Jesus. I remember the moment she came up out of the water. She felt the presence of God to such a strong degree that she began crying uncontrollably. She held tightly to her aunt and uncle, apologizing to them for mocking their Christianity in her younger years.

Miracles, small and large, can take place like this when people are baptized.

You know, it sometimes seems as though we have a choice as to whether or not we'll be baptized, because not all Christians choose to follow this command. But the truth is, if we've made a commitment to obey God in everything, why would we choose to not obey his command to be baptized? It simply doesn't make sense.

If you're reading *New Life in Jesus* as a part of a Bible study group, and you want to be baptized, you can ask whether the leader, or maybe even their pastor, would be willing to baptize you. For those of you reading this book on your own, maybe it will work out best to be baptized once you begin attending a church.

And speaking of church, there are some basics to know which will help you as you begin your friendship with God. I *could* suggest that your growth as a follower of Jesus depends on your ability to read the Bible, pray, go to church, serve others, and share your faith. I could, but it isn't true. Your growth as a Christian depends on your interaction with the Holy Spirit, your connection to him... as you read the Bible, as you pray, as you go to church, as you serve, as you share your faith, and so much more.

As I close, I want to say a few words about the fact that you've felt the tug of God on your heart and have responded by praying your own prayer to be born again.

The Bible teaches that "if we confess Jesus as Lord and believe in our heart that God raised him from the dead, we will be saved" (Romans 10:9). This is a rock-solid promise from God. You will never again have to decide whether or not you want to be born again, but every day you will have to choose to live the life that you've been given. In the next chapter we'll talk more about salvation and what happens next.

Until then, I would suggest starting to get to know your Savior better. You can do this by reading one of the biographies of Jesus in the Bible: Matthew, Mark, Luke, or John. Personally, I recommend the Gospel of John, and after that, the Book of Romans. Each time, as you begin to read, ask the Holy Spirit to teach you. Ask him to speak to you. You'll begin to see your friendship take shape in no time.

I'd like to end my comments with a prayer for you.

Dear God,

Thank you for the message of a reconciled relationship with you. Thank you for salvation through Jesus in the face of emptiness and eternal death.

Lord, I ask on behalf of this person who has prayed to receive new life in Jesus, that you would fill them with the power of your Holy Spirit. I pray that he would speak to them clearly and that he would protect them from the negative words that are bound to be spoken by those who don't yet know you. Let this person's new life and words draw those around them into a friendship with you as well.

Give this new friend of yours a strong desire to read the Bible, to know more about Jesus, and to learn more about the new person they themselves are destined to become.

Thank you so much, Jesus.

In your name I pray. Amen.

Chapter 4—
SPIRIT, SOUL, AND BODY
How is friendship with God experienced?

Although we are 'saved' only once in our life, salvation began when the Holy Spirit came to live in us and made us alive in Christ. The salvation of our soul develops over our lifetime as we respond in faith to everything the Holy Spirit communicates. And salvation will culminate when Jesus returns and our body is changed to be like his.

* * *

The Guy from the Carport

Early in our marriage, when my wife and I were still living in our apartment, there was a young couple who parked next to us under the carport. From time to time we would see each other there and say hi, but that's about as far as it went.

I was working temporary jobs at the time and one of my assignments was for a company that had a major and immediate project coming up. But the project didn't materialize during the few days I was there. As I waited for glitches to be ironed out, the only thing I accomplished was... meeting and visiting briefly with Wayne, the guy from the carport. I thought it was quite a coincidence that he worked there.

Once I moved on to my next job assignment, our relationship went back to the crossing of paths as one of us was leaving home and the other was returning; although now I could say, "Hi, *Wayne*."

Several months went by, and one day, as we were pulling into the carport, Wayne was pacing the sidewalk. He had a nervous look in his eye as he walked up to me and said, "The Holy Spirit told me to talk to you."

Wayne began sharing with me that he was a Christian whose life was spiraling out of control.

He and I spent a lot of time together over the next few weeks. I listened as a confused and sometimes angry man tried to make sense out of things that were happening in his life. I did my best to support and encourage him when I could.

Wayne joined us as we hosted a Christian book study with another couple. We were reading and discussing a book[1] which had impacted my wife and me.

Through our discussions I realized that, although Wayne had experienced salvation through Jesus, he didn't understand salvation. And his lack of understanding actually contributed to the negative turn his life had taken.

Over time, as he began to understand the truth of what it means to be a saved person, the fog began to lift from Wayne's mind. He took the message to heart and began sharing it with others. His confidence grew. He began to hear God's voice clearly again. Ultimately, through a series of incredible and, quite frankly, miraculous personal events, God restored the life that had been slipping away from Wayne. It was a wonderful outcome to his story.

As I think about the story, though, I can't seem to shake this statement: "Although he had experienced salvation, he didn't understand it; and it had a negative effect in his life." I've seen this story of Wayne's play out in the lives of others as well.

I guess there are any number of reasons why people have chosen to become Christians. I've heard good answers; like "to go to heaven," and "to change my life around and get my wife back." But rarely do I hear the reason that God had in mind when he decided to offer us salvation in the first place; that is, to begin and develop a personal relationship with him. Although many of us have heard the phrase 'personal relationship with Jesus Christ,' few of us have ever been taught what it means. We've barely even seen what it looks like.

Hopefully, you've seen enough in this book to begin to realize that a relationship with God is a series of 'God experiences.' He answers prayer, he teaches, he sets people free, he speaks and calls people to serve, he saves and protects, he leads people back to himself, and that's just for starters.

The time has come for us to add knowledge to our experience of salvation, so that we can also add the on-going experiences of a relationship with God. In doing this, we will see the connection between the sixth, seventh, and eighth

Great Wonders: "People, Born Again"; "God's People Live by Faith"; and "God and His People, Together Forever."

Not Exactly *Me, Myself, and I*

I've witnessed the moment that the teaching in this chapter clicks in the heart and mind of person after person. I've seen it in their eyes.

One Sunday morning, I had my big chance to share this lesson with a crowd of about 75 or so. I had three members of the church's drama team behind me, wearing T-shirts I had made. Kathy wore a white shirt with the word *SPIRIT* on the front. Aaron stood next to her wearing a gray shirt with the word *SOUL*. And next to him was Ken in a black shirt with the word *BODY*. As I gave the talk that morning, these three actors demonstrated the connection, the struggle, and the salvation of our spirit, soul, and body.

Now I love success stories. Unfortunately, this isn't exactly one of them. I completely blew my opportunity that morning. Convinced I absolutely knew my material inside and out, I chose not to prepare an outline. I was "shot-gunning it," as one of the actors told me later. I was so all-over-the-place I actually heard the Holy Spirit say, *You're done*, as if I was being pulled off the stage with a long hook. And yet, several people told me afterward that the teaching had answered questions for them that no one had ever addressed before. So I know that this teaching can be impacting for people, and maybe more so, if I bury my ego and follow an outline.

The first thing I want to do is to identify the spirit, soul, and body—which sounds easy enough. Then, we're going to look at how salvation affects the three parts of every person at different times and in different ways. Finally, we're going to see why this concept is so powerfully relevant to people like my neighbor Wayne, and to you and me as well.

Okay. That's a good outline to follow.

In the Bible, two distinct concepts define a human being: *outer appearance* and *inner self*. The word *body*, of course, is used most often to refer to our outer appearance. And two words, *soul* and *spirit*, are commonly used to define our inner self.

I've heard soul and spirit described as conjoined twins. Just as it takes intricate surgery to separate conjoined siblings, the Bible indicates that the separation of the soul and spirit is also intricate, and can only be accomplished by God's Word[2].

Together, my dad and I once studied these two words in Greek, the original language of the New Testament, to see if there's any distinction between them. This is almost the entire extent of my knowledge of the Bible's original languages, so don't get nervous. Here's the essence of what I see on our five pages of notes, torn from a spiral notebook.

- The Greek word *psuchē* (pronounced *soo-khay'*) means 'breath, the soul.' We identified 36 occurrences in the New Testament as the word *life* and 33 occurrences as the word *soul*. Our notes are fairly cut and dry. Dad summarized it pretty well when he wrote at the bottom of a page; *person—personality—life—self—soul—the real you!*

- *Pneuma* (pronounced *nyoo'-mah*) means 'wind, spirit.' We identified 239 occurrences that referred to the Holy Spirit (God) and 103 occurrences that referred to the human spirit. The notes we jotted down are much more dynamic. For a Christian (an important distinction), the human spirit is the offspring of the Holy Spirit[3]. It's described as the spirit of an adopted child[4]. The human spirit worships God[5], and is provoked by idol worship[6]. It rejoices greatly[7]. Not only does it pray[8]; it's ready, willing, and eager to watch and pray[9]. The human spirit serves God[10], and a fervent spirit causes us to speak and teach about Jesus[11].

Dad and I drew the conclusion that the word *spirit* strongly implies a 'godly self' and *soul* speaks more of a 'personal self,' although the differences weren't always black and white—bringing the idea of conjoined back to mind.

At one of the national bookstore chains I noticed a selection of books and DVDs labeled *Mind, Spirit, and Body.* And it dawned on me; each part of our humanity has a lot to do with healthy relationships. So, based on what we discovered about these words from the Bible, here are some definitions I want to establish, not only for the chapter, but for the entire *8 Great Wonders* teaching.

- ***Spirit***—our godly self. We were created *spiritually* to experience friendship with God.

From time to time, I listen to a radio program that's hosted by two atheists who talk politics more than religion. I once heard these two men laughing about their inability to find the spirit inside them—"whatever that is," one of them mocked. Ironic, isn't it? The human spirit is meant to enjoy a relationship with God, which atheists can't experience.

- **Soul**—our personal self. We were created *personally* to enjoy healthy relationships with other people. I like to describe the soul as *emotion, personality* and *intellect*, but many other words also apply; like *heart, mind, will, thought, conscience, comprehension*—the list goes on and on.

How we treat others is incredibly important. People, I feel, are the most valuable thing on earth. And the best things about people are the experiences we can share and the stories we can tell.

- **Body**—our physical self with its five senses: sight, hearing, touch, taste, and smell. We were created *physically* to enjoy and responsibly care for God's creation.

The human body is built to experience the goodness of the world around it in a healthy manner. In general, how we treat the earth, the water, and the air is as important as how we care for our own backyard gardens and family pets. And caring for our own bodies through nutrition and an active lifestyle can enhance every relationship we experience.

Each of us is made up of spirit, soul, and body. These three words appear in the Bible hundreds of times, but interestingly, there's only one verse in which we see all three together.

*Now may the God of peace Himself sanctify you entirely;
and may your spirit and soul and body be preserved
complete, without blame at the coming of our Lord Jesus
Christ.*   *—1 Thessalonians 5:23*

"Complete, without blame." Think about that for a moment.

The very first time I shared the *8 Great Wonders* teaching from our workbook, it was as a part of my daughter's school lessons. I remember her question, "Are there any people alive right now who are related to Adam and Eve?" She was amazed to learn that we're *all* related to Adam and Eve.

And what a wonderful thing; perfect friendship with God, perfect relationships with one another, and responsible care for the world around them. This is where we come from. This is our heritage as human beings, the family of Adam and Eve.

If you took the opportunity to read *The What-Could-Have-Been Bible* mentioned in Chapter 1, you probably noticed that where we came from is also where we're meant to go. The question is: How do we get there from where we are now?

Completely, More Each Day, and Not Yet

Let's begin a conversation about how we experience salvation. And let's start with a picture of the health and wholeness that comes from a personal relationship with God. It's a picture of six connected links: God the Father, Jesus Christ, and the Holy Spirit... *connected to...* a person's spirit, soul, and body.

We have to start here, with the three parts of every person, to understand salvation and the relationship we're meant to experience.

There's no such thing as a completely whole person outside of a relationship with God. And there's no such thing as a relationship with God unless our spirit is born again, which reconnects us to God through the Holy Spirit.

I heard about a country preacher who had an interesting response to the question, "Are you saved?" His answer was, "Completely, more and more each day, and not yet." He understood that biblical salvation affects the spirit, soul, and body of a person in different ways and at different times.

Being born again, reconnected to the Holy Spirit, points to our initial need for salvation. Remember Romans 6:6? *Our old self was crucified with Christ.* How many of us are born into this world already knowing God personally? The answer is none of us. Although God is right here with us, there's no connection to him because of the deadness inside us. Everything about biblical salvation points first to our spirit's need to be born of God. That's why Jesus said that we "must be born again" (John 3:3), because "that which is born of the Holy Spirit is spirit" (John 3:6).

Our spirit experiences a *moment* of salvation. Being born of God is instantaneous and complete. The scholarly word is *regeneration.* And it happens because the Holy Spirit comes to live in the new Christian. John, one of Jesus' Apostles, tells us in one of his writings that "no one who is born of God practices sin, because God's seed remains in him, and he cannot sin because he is born of God" (1 John 3:9). *God's seed*, mentioned here, is our spirit. Paul taught that, with the new birth, comes a new identity. We actually "become the righteousness of God in Christ" (2 Corinthians 5:21). This is also a reference to our spirit.

So, our spirit experiences salvation first.

Next, beginning at the moment of spiritual salvation and continuing through the remainder of our life, our soul can experience a *process* of salvation. Paul would refer to this as 'becoming like Jesus as our thinking and behavior are changed[12].' The scholarly word is *sanctification*. This happens as we approach spiritual disciplines—reading the Bible, praying, attending church, etc.—with an expectancy to hear, believe, and obey the Holy Spirit. Over time, as we experience a friendship with God in this way, he develops our character and reveals our calling in life. Although the process is simple, it's not always easy. When it feels as if I'm taking 'two steps forward and one step, *or more*, back,' that's when I find some of the *Principles of a Wonderful Trip* from Chapter 1 very helpful. It's good for me to see those again from time to time.

So, our spirit can be born again in a moment, and our soul can be developed over time to become more and more like Jesus. But there's even more good news. Our body can also be saved.

No one has experienced the salvation of the body... yet. But God has promised that the Holy Spirit living inside us is a guarantee of our physical salvation[13]. Our body will experience this finalizing salvation, so to speak, the moment Jesus returns for us[14]. Our body will be made perfect, immortal, and incorruptible[15], just like it was when Adam walked in the Garden of Eden and when Jesus walked from the empty tomb. The scholarly word is *glorification*.

Although I've just described three parts to salvation, touching the three parts of every person, there's a Greek word that pulls all of this together in one wonderful package. The word is sōzō (pronounced *sode'-zo*), which means 'made whole.' If you and I choose to believe God's message and begin a loving relationship with him, then it's God's agenda for us to be completely restored—spirit, soul, and body. What an incredible thought.

The Battle for 'Undecided'

As we head down the home stretch, I want to make sure that we understand something. What we've talked about so far is all well and good, but it isn't relevant yet. It won't impact us until we know how to bring these truths into our lives so that they can make a difference when we wake up tomorrow morning. Please follow me for a few more minutes.

In a debate, the three most important participants are the two debaters and the person who hasn't made up his or her mind yet—also known, during election years, as 'Undecided.' During a debate, the two presenters aren't trying to convince one another of their positions. And they aren't really trying to pull audience members who hold the opposite view over to their way of thinking. The goal of a good debater is to appeal to Mr. or Ms. Undecided.

I understood this the night I attended a debate between a Christian and an atheist. The atheist said that he wouldn't consider himself to be an atheist, he was just someone who *doubted* the existence of the Christian God. When he said this, I prayed a silent prayer of protection for all the Christians in the audience who could identify with his statement, who struggle with doubt.

Sometimes living as a Christian can seem like a struggle because of the debate; not the publicized one at the venue down the street, but the debate inside of us every day of our lives.

Ken and I met over breakfast one morning. (Yes, the same Ken who would later act out these principles with Kathy and Aaron.) That morning, he confessed some of his darkest struggles with sin. He told me that he had accepted Christ as his Savior when he was a child. And he said that, growing up in church, he knew all the teachings and practices of Christianity. But, like Wayne in the story which opened this chapter, Ken was a Christian whose life was out of control. In his own words[16]:

I'm a person who has had a roller coaster ride in my relationship with God since I can remember. I'm a person who wishes he could just find out what it is he's supposed to do with his life and be happy about it. I'm a person who's afraid to be alone with his thoughts. I'm a person who's so consumed with his sin that it inhibits me from being who God has called me to be.

Am I doomed to the life I'm now in? Is there a way out? Where would I be if I followed what God had laid out for me for the past 10 to 15 years? One thing is absolutely certain—I cannot continue down the road I am currently on. My depression and sin will only increase, and I will end up an old man wondering where my life went. I don't ever want to play the 'what if' game. Unfortunately, I already am.

Quite honestly, it was an emotional moment for both of us as Ken described his depression and the sin which led to it. I respectfully asked for and was given permission to respond. So I set three juice glasses in front of us. "This first one is our spirit. This next one is our soul. And this last one is our body."

Here's what I shared.

At the near end of the three glasses is our born-again spirit. It cannot sin. It embraces everything that God communicates.

At the far end is our body, or "the flesh" as the Bible refers to it. It's selfish and cannot do right. The flesh is driven by what it sees, hears, touches, tastes, and smells. And as much as our spirit is the righteousness of God, our flesh is the wretchedness of man.

Stuck in the middle, being pulled by both the spirit and the flesh, is our soul, which has some decisions to make.

For those who are according to the flesh set their minds on the things of the flesh, but those who are according to the Spirit, the things of the Spirit. —Romans 8:5

I made sure that Ken understood that *fleshly-minded* is when our soul bases decisions on the urges of the body and its five senses. Whether it's deviant behavior, addictive vices, or simple selfishness, the mission statement of the flesh is this: *If it feels good, do it.*

Being *spiritually-minded* is when the soul makes decisions based on the communication between the Holy Spirit and our spirit. *If it's God's will, do it.*

⁶For the mind set on the flesh is death, but the mind set on the Spirit is life and peace, ⁷because the mind set on the flesh is hostile toward God; for it does not subject itself to the law of God, for it is not even able to do so, ⁸and those who are in the flesh cannot please God.

⁹However, you are not in the flesh but in the Spirit, if indeed the Spirit of God dwells in you. But if anyone does not have the Spirit of Christ, he does not belong to Him. ¹⁰If Christ is in you, though the body is dead because of sin, yet the spirit is alive because of righteousness. ¹¹But if the Spirit of Him who raised Jesus from the dead dwells in you, He who raised Christ Jesus from the dead will also give life to your mortal bodies through His Spirit who dwells in you.

¹²So then, brethren, we are under obligation, not to the flesh, to live according to the flesh—¹³for if you are living according to the flesh, you must die; but if by the Spirit you are putting to death the deeds of the body, you will live. ¹⁴For all who are being led by the Spirit of God, these are sons of God. ¹⁵For you have not received a spirit of slavery leading to fear again, but you have received a spirit of adoption as sons by which we cry out, "Abba! Father!" ¹⁶The Spirit Himself testifies with our spirit that we are children of God, ¹⁷and if children, heirs also, heirs of God and fellow heirs with Christ, if indeed we suffer with Him so that we may also be glorified with Him. —Romans 8:6–17

Somewhere between the hopelessness of Ken's journal entry and the profound hope of Romans 8 is where the reality of our daily lives seems to exist. Have you ever heard anything like this? "And that guy calls himself a Christian! Good Christians don't do things like that."

Before we became a Christian, being fleshly-minded was all we knew. Every one of our decisions was based on what we saw, heard, touched, tasted, and smelled. For those who come to Christ at an early age, there may not be years and years of life experiences that were fleshly, but for others there may be decades of *stinkin' thinkin'* that have to be overcome. Thankfully, according to Romans 8, which we just read, it can be.

What I'm about to describe may sound far-fetched, but it's based on principles from Scripture. It's a scene from our own lives.

Satan, "the serpent of old[17]," tempts us to commit sin. Despite the fact that we know better—maybe we look around to make sure no one sees us—we do it. Immediately, Satan accuses us. He points us out to God[18], and says, "Look! Your *child* is betraying you. You couldn't possibly love a sinner like that." He whispers something similar into our ear as well.

But Jesus Christ is also standing there. The Bible calls him our intercessor[19]—our defense lawyer, so to speak. He shows God the Father the nail scars in his wrists, and says, "The death penalty for sin has already been paid."

God brings down the gavel against Satan's accusation, and declares us "Not guilty![20]" (We Christians love a story like this, don't we?)

As Satan slams down his briefcase and curses his way out of the courtroom, our heavenly Father calls Jesus over for a private talk. "Tell my child to stop it![21]"

Hear that last statement again. *"Tell my child to stop it!"*

Jesus communicates God's will to us through the Holy Spirit, and the next thing you know we're feeling very uneasy about our sin. Not condemned to die, but convicted to repent.

God very strongly wants us to stop following our fleshly desires and to start obeying the Holy Spirit.

Just stop it. Just say no. Doesn't this sound wonderful and easy? You and I know it's not that easy at all. We know that the flesh isn't going to go away. No matter how *perfectly* spiritual we would like to become, our flesh will never lay down and die. The battle between the spirit and the flesh is rough and on-going. But, thank God, the Holy Spirit will never give up on speaking God's character, his heart, and his will into our lives.

It's not enough that we know how all this works. "Knowing this" isn't going to change our lives; not until we change our minds and yield to God. Truthfully, *how much* and *how fast* we grow as a Christian is directly tied to how often we say 'yes' to the Holy Spirit and 'no' to our selfish, sinful desires.

If we become a 'continual yes' to the Holy Spirit[22], we will see him develop our character and reveal our calling in life. And that's the key to everything.

So, let's make up our minds that we're going to open the Bible, and pray, and hang out with God's people, and serve others, and share our faith with others—all with the purpose of experiencing the God who calls us into this personal relationship with him. Let's be intentional about experiencing God.

As we wake up each morning we can pray a powerful prayer: *Lord, fill me with the power of your Holy Spirit today.* We can pray it because we want the strength in our lives to come in the area of our spiritual-mindedness, not our fleshliness. And we can pray it because God wants us to grow up and become like Christ.

For those whom [God] foreknew, He also predestined to become conformed to the image of His Son, so that He would be the firstborn among many brethren; ...

Sometimes, I can actually feel a strong sense of 'something' behind this message and I have to remember that it can be a bit overwhelming for people. I asked Ken if he was okay, but I could see it in his eyes.

"After 20 years of being saved," he said, "I have hope for the first time that Christ can save me from my sinful body, and that it will happen through my relationship with God."

Before he left that morning, Ken told me, "If people could see what I've just seen, their lives would be absolutely transformed."

Based on my own life and the lives of others I've known, I would have to agree.

Afterword—
CHECKING AND RECHECKING THE CONNECTIONS

Not too long ago, someone reminded me of one of those everyday truths in life: "When there's a 'disconnect' in the system, go back to the beginning and check each one of the components, until the problem is revealed." No big deal, right?

As soon as I heard it, something clicked inside me, as though God had taken a highlighter to it. *Keep this in mind. It's important.*

Before the end of the day, that reminder led me to an important discovery about the lessons behind each of the *8 Great Wonders*. These biblical teachings can and should be used as gauges in judging whether or not our friendship with God is developing. So every now and then, let's come back and ask ourselves the following questions:

God Created People

Am I convinced that God's purpose is for all people to know him and be with him? Am I living in God's purpose for me (specifically, as well as generally)? Am I compelled to share God's purpose for all people with those who don't know Him yet?

People Sinned Against God

Am I convinced that Adam's sin and separation from God have been passed down to all people? Do I feel any kind of distance between God and me, which may be caused by sin in my life? Am I compelled to tell others that feeling distant and having doubts about God stem from being separated from Him by sin?

God's Law Condemned Sinners

Am I convinced that God's Law judges all people to be sinners and sentences us to death? Do I feel uncomfortable, even defensive or ashamed, around churches, the Bible, or growing Christians? Am I compelled to tell others how guilt and shame come from us "falling short" of God's standard for our lives?

Jesus Christ Died for Sinners

Am I convinced that everyone was "crucified with Christ," although God reconciled us to himself and forgave us the day Jesus died? Am I living "dead to sin," reconciled to God, and forgiven because I know what Jesus accomplished for me on the cross? Am I compelled to share the message of God's love with those who don't yet know that they were "crucified with Christ" and need to be born again?

Jesus, Alive Again!

Am I convinced that hope for empty and lifeless people can only come from someone who has risen from the dead? Am I living as someone who believes that, "if anyone can give me abundant life, the living Jesus can"? Am I compelled to share hopeful and encouraging stories with others about Jesus being alive and living in me?

People, Born Again

Am I convinced that, when anyone repents and believes in the gospel, the Holy Spirit comes to live in them and raises them to new life? Do I believe that, having been born again, I am a literal child of God and can hear his voice? Am I compelled to look for opportunities with people in which I can share the gospel of Jesus and a personal relationship with him?

God's People Live by Faith

Am I convinced that faith is a response of belief and obedience—the only right response—to everything the Holy Spirit says to me? Do I create 'opportunities for faith' by asking the Holy Spirit to speak to me when I read the Bible, pray, and spend time with growing Christians? Am I compelled to back up the words I share with non-Christians by living a life that pleases God?

God and His People, Together Forever

Am I convinced that Jesus will return someday, and that he will judge and reward his people for how they lived? Is my desire to live each day in such a way as to hear Jesus say, "Well done, good and faithful servant. Inherit the kingdom prepared for you"? Am I compelled to share with both non-Christians and Christians that knowing and being with God is possible not only in eternity but here today as well?

ENDNOTES

Chapter 1—Creation and Forever

[1] John Crudele, CSP

[2] *Jesus Verbs*:

    Believe me—John 5:25–47;

    Follow me—John 1:43; Matthew 4:19/Mark 1:17; Matthew 9:9/Mark 2:14/Luke 5:27; Luke 9:23; Matthew 16:24/Mark 8:34; Matthew 8:22/Luke 9:59; Matthew 19:21/Mark 10:21; John 12:26; John 21:19, 22;

    Practice the truth—John 3:21;

    Worship—John 4:23–24;

    Let your light shine—Matthew 5:16;

    Freely give—Matthew 9:8;

    Love me—John 14:15;

    Keep my word—John 14:23;

Pray and Fast—Matthew 6:5–18;

Ask/Seek/Knock—Matthew 7:7–11;

Take courage—John 16:33;

Come to me—Matthew 11:28–30;

Hear my words/Act on them—Luke 6:47–48;

Forgive—Luke 17:3–4; Mark 11:25;

Take up your cross—Matthew 10:38; Luke 9:23–24; Matthew 16:24/Mark 8:34–35;

Humble yourself—Matthew 18:4; Luke 14:11; Luke 18:14; Matthew 23:12;

Hear my voice—John 10:27–28;

Serve others—Mark 9:35; Matthew 23:10–11; Luke 22:25–27; John 13:12–17;

Count the cost—Luke 14:26–33;

Keep watching and praying—Matthew 26:41/Mark 14:38;

Receive the Holy Spirit—John 20:22;

Shepherd my sheep—John 21:15–17;

Go/Preach/Make disciples/Baptize them/Teach them— Matthew 28:19–20

[3] Special thanks to Rick Loy (the minister who baptized his friend and Charlie's) for refreshing my memory and filling in gaps in the story.

[4] The *Romans Road* is a path of scriptures which has led many to accept God's free gift of salvation. I noted the following version in my Bible when I was in high school: First, Romans 3:10, then Romans 3:23, Romans 5:12, Romans 6:23, Revelation 20:14–15, Romans 5:8, Romans 10:13, and 1 John 5:11–13.

[5] Genesis 2:10

[6] Revelation 22:1

Chapter 2—Separated, Judged, and Crucified

1 *"The serpent was the craftiest animal ... that it could make her wise."* Based on Genesis 3:1–6a.

2 This statement is based on Genesis 3:8a.

3 William Ernest Henley's poem, "Invictus," is in the public domain.

4 Romans 1:18–20

5 Romans 1:21–32

6 Romans 3:23

7 Genesis 3:24

8 A press release entitled "Attorney General Statement Regarding Timothy McVeigh," dated May 24th, 2001, reads, in-part: "This particular investigation produced millions of records, including millions of pages of hotel, motel or phone records, over 238,000 photographs, over 28,000 reports of interviews, and more than 23,000 pieces of evidence."

9 Romans 15:20

10 2 Corinthians 11:23

11 Romans 6:5–6, Romans 7:4, 2 Corinthians 5:13–14, Galatians 2:20, Galatians 6:14, Colossians 2:20, 2 Timothy 2:11, 1 Peter 2:24

12 Bob George, Classic Christianity: Life's Too Short to Miss the Real Thing (Eugene: Harvest House, 1989).

Chapter 3—Crucifixion and Resurrection

1 Matthew 6:9–13

2 Matthew 14:15–21, Mark 6:34–44, Luke 9:12–17, John 6:5–14

3 Luke 10:30–37

4 Luke 15:11–32

5 Matthew 1:18–25

6 M. R. DeHaan, The Chemistry of the Blood and Other
   Stirring Messages (Grand Rapids: Zondervan, 1943), 31.

Chapter 4—Spirit, Soul, and Body

1 Bob George, Classic Christianity: Life's Too Short to Miss the
   Real Thing (Eugene: Harvest House, 1989).

2 Hebrews 4:12

3 John 3:6

4 Romans 8:15

5 John 4:23

6 Acts 17:16

7 Luke 1:47

8 Ephesians 6:18

9 Matthew 26:41

10 Romans 1:9

11 Acts 18:25

12 Romans 8:29, Romans 12:2

13 Ephesians 1:13–14

14 1 John 3:2

15 1 Corinthians 15:51–53

16 *"I'm a person who … Unfortunately, I already am."* Edited
   from an entry in Ken's journal and used with permission.

17 Revelation 12:9

18 Revelation 12:10

19 Romans 8:34, Hebrews 7:25

20 Romans 8:33

21 John 16:8–13

22 See Romans 12:1

* * *

Years ago, when work began on the 8 Great Wonders *Bible study book, the first pieces written were light-hearted news articles based on the 'original' headlines. So, just for fun...*

GOD CREATES PEOPLE

Garden of Eden—After creating airborne and aquatic animals yesterday, God continued to display his mastery of the physical sciences this morning by creating land animals. The highlight of this sixth day of creation came later when God created a man, after deciding to do so in his own likeness. God and the man, named Adam, spent quite a while together, as the man was allowed to give names to all the animals. As evening came, God caused Adam to fall asleep. He removed one of Adam's ribs and formed it into a woman—to be a helper and mate. A spokesman for God said that he and his favorite couple are enjoying themselves completely, and that God is now ready for a day off.   *Full Story—Genesis 1 & 2*

PEOPLE SIN AGAINST GOD

East of Eden—Details are sketchy, but something seems to have gone very wrong in paradise. The Garden of Eden was shut down this afternoon as God met with Adam, Eve and a serpent behind closed doors. A short while later, Adam and his wife were escorted out of the garden. A heavily-armed angel has since been seen standing guard at the garden's entrance. The distraught couple has now gone into seclusion, but reporters were able to speak with them briefly as they were leaving. Adam reportedly commented, "God gave her to me, and then she tricked me." At that point, Eve is said to have responded sharply, "Don't blame me. I'm the victim here." The serpent has not been seen since the meeting with God. God's spokesman said that, "at least for the time being, he's not talking to any of you." *Full Story—Genesis 3*

GOD'S LAW IS GIVEN

Mt. Sinai—For the third time in as many days, Israel's leader, Moses, has met directly with God himself. In the two prior meetings, the pair discussed preparations for God's spectacular appearance today. As morning broke, lightning, thunder and trumpet blasts announced God's arrival. Moses brought his people to the base of the mountain where they nervously looked on. Moses then spent quite a while on the mountain's summit as he met with God. He returned some time later with two stone tablets said to contain God's laws in God's handwriting. However, during his absence, a small but unruly crowd had forced Moses' brother to forge a false god for them. (Ironically, it is reported that God's first Law is, "You must have no other gods before me.") When Moses returned and saw the idol, he hurled the tablets at the unruly crowd. Leaders have now killed about 3000 of the lawbreakers.   *Full Story—Exodus 19–32*

JESUS CHRIST DIES

Outside Jerusalem—Never before has a Roman execution attracted so much public attention. Jesus of Nazareth, a self-styled Jewish teacher, was crucified under Roman authority today. However, Governor Pontius Pilate has rejected responsibility for the punishment. Jewish leaders arrested their criminal late last night and released him into Roman hands early this morning. The man was accused of claiming he was God, a highly unusual accusation to deserve death. A Roman soldier present at the execution said that he thought the man to be the Son of God, but few of the local citizens in the crowd that gathered throughout the afternoon shared the opinion. Authorities had begun to weigh their options for crowd control when the afternoon sky began to turn as black as night, sending the crowd back to their homes. Sources indicate that this seemed to be about the same time that Jesus succumbed to death.

Full Story—Matthew 27, Mark 15, Luke 23, John 19

JESUS, ALIVE AGAIN!

Outside Jerusalem—Very early this morning, controversy erupted when the tomb containing the dead body of Jesus of Nazareth was found empty. Several Jewish women, friends of the deceased, arrived at the empty tomb to carry out Jewish burial customs. They said they found Roman guards asleep at the site, a crime punishable by death. The guards could not be reached for comment. How the body was removed remains a mystery. The guards had been placed at the tomb because Jewish leaders worried something like this was going to happen. Sources say Jesus told people openly before he died that he would be raised from the dead. Rumors already abound that this is exactly what took place in the wee hours of the morning.

Full Story—Matthew 28, Mark 16, Luke 24, John 20

your name ACCEPTS SALVATION

Editorial—I don't remember which of the trivia games it was, but a number of years ago I pulled a card that asked, "What is the name of the song played at the end of every Billy Graham religious service?" I guessed the only religious tune I knew, *Amazing Grace*. The funny thing about the question and my answer, I was familiar with both, yet understood neither. Like most people, especially in Western culture, I'd seen Billy Graham on television. I'd seen people pour from the stands at his call to receive Jesus Christ as their personal Lord and Savior. Of course, I wasn't paying attention to the song they were singing in the background. Each time, I watched and said to myself, "What are those people thinking!"—or singing, in regard to *Amazing Grace*. Actually, I wasn't even sure it was a religious song. More than once I'd heard it sung in a pub. Much has changed since then. I now know that *Just As I Am* is the song that is sung after a Billy Graham message. I also know what people are thinking when they respond to a call to accept Christ into their heart and life, and I know what's so amazing about grace because I've experienced it for myself. Have you?   *Related Story—Acts 2*

Editorial—How many George Bailey's do you know? George Bailey, of course, is the name of the central character in the movie *It's a Wonderful Life*. George's sense of personal purpose was second only to his willingness to put others ahead of himself. I've been asking myself lately, "What makes a good Christian?" The more I think about it, the more George Bailey's name comes to mind. So who is it that you know personally who exhibits a strong sense of personal purpose and vision? Who do you know who is willing, maybe even driven, to put the interests of other people ahead of their own? There is, of course, something more to being a good Christian than just being a servant-leader. Ask yourself, does the George (or Georgette) Bailey I know follow the direct leading of God in his or her life? If so, your friend is an example of a good Christian, with a wonderful life. Are you?

Related Story—Acts 3–5

GOD AND PEOPLE, TOGETHER FOREVER

Mt. Olivet—Science-fiction writers could not have crafted a more incredible story than what the world has been witnessing over these last several years. Seemingly every individual who disappeared without a trace a few years ago returned to Earth today, riding white horses with Jesus Christ, the King of kings and Lord of lords. Jesus returned to earth about 2000 years after his followers claim he ascended into heaven after rising from the dead. Doubters were silenced once and for all at his appearance. Christ returned as hostile military maneuvers were taking place in the Valley of Megiddo. The nation of Israel was on high alert at the time, the leaders having called for a National Day of Prayer for Deliverance. Jesus Christ came to their rescue like he was the answer to their prayers. One can only wonder what the future holds now.   *Full Story—Revelation 19–22*

ANOTHER WONDER IDENTIFIED?

Jerusalem—Could it be that there are nine fine wonders in human history? In an upper conference room, it was announced today that the headline *God's Holy Spirit Is Given* should be identified as the sixth of nine wonders in God's history with people. Supporters of the nine wonders theory suggested that "the outpouring of the Holy Spirit, 50 days after Christ's resurrection, qualifies as a wonder, being an event from history, which can impact the lives of every human being." The new headline was compared to "God's Law Is Given." Experts pointed out that "only the indwelling Holy Spirit can accomplish what people had hoped God's Law would do in their lives." They summed up their presentation by stating that "the outpouring of God's Spirit bridges the gap between Christ's rising from the dead and any individual's acceptance of the free gift of salvation." The author of *The 8 Great Wonders of Human History* offered no comment, but was seen scratching his head.

Made in the USA
Middletown, DE
18 September 2016